AMERICAN FOLKSONGS

FOR EASY GUITAR

72 Favorite Songs from the Frontiers

ISBN 978-0-7935-6952-6

HAL•LEONARD® CORPORATION

7777 W. BLUEMOUND RD. P.O. BOX 13819 MILWAUKEE, WI 53213

Visit Hal Leonard Online at www.halleonard.com

AMERICAN FOLKSONGS

FOR EASY GUITAR

72 Favorite Songs from the Frontiers of America

STRUM AND PICK PATTERNS

This chart contains the suggested strum and pick patterns that are referred to by number at the beginning of each song in this book. The symbols ⊓ and ∨ in the strum patterns refer to down and up strokes, respectively. The letters in the pick patterns indicate which right-hand fingers plays which strings.

p = thumb
i = index finger
m = middle finger
a = ring finger

For example; Pick Pattern 2
is played: thumb - index - middle - ring

Strum Patterns   Pick Patterns

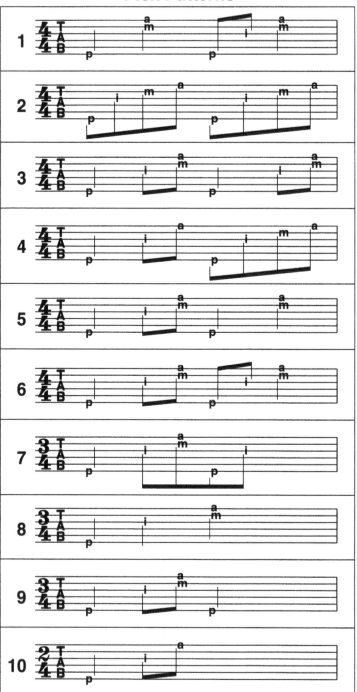

You can use the 3/4 Strum or Pick Patterns in songs written in compound meter (6/8, 9/8, 12/8, etc.). For example, you can accompany a song in 6/8 by playing the 3/4 pattern twice in each measure. The 4/4 Strum and Pick Patterns can be used for songs written in cut time (¢) by doubling the note time values in the patterns. Each pattern would therefore last two measures in cut time.

All My Trials

Traditional Spiritual

Strum Pattern: 4
Pick Pattern: 5

Verse
Freely

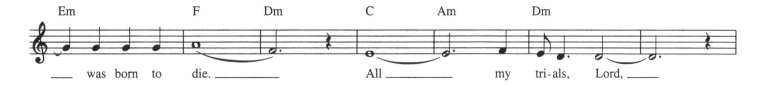

1. Hush, lit-tle ba-by, don't you cry, _____ you know your ma-ma _____
2., 3. *See Additional Lyrics*

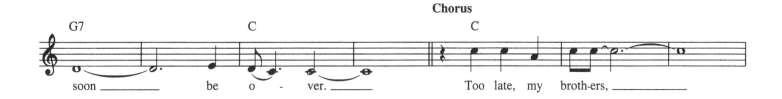

_____ was born to die. _____ All _____ my tri-als, Lord, _____

Chorus

soon _____ be o-ver. _____ Too late, my broth-ers, _____

too late, _____ but nev-er mind. _____ All _____ my

tri-als, Lord, _____ soon _____ be o-ver. _____

Additional Lyrics

2. If religion was a thing money could buy,
   The rich would live and the poor would die.

3. I had a little book that was given to me,
   And ev'ry page spelled liberty.

All the Pretty Little Horses

Traditional

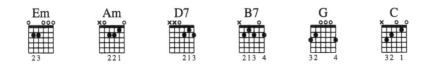

Strum Pattern: 4
Pick Pattern: 5

Verse
Moderately

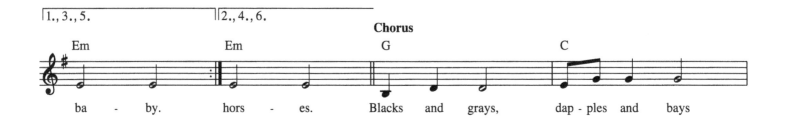

1. Hush - a - bye, don't you cry, go to sleep - y lit - tle
When you wake you shall have all the pret - ty lit - tle
2., 3. *See Additional Lyrics*

1., 3., 5. *2., 4., 6.*

Chorus

ba - by. hors - es. Blacks and grays, dap - ples and bays

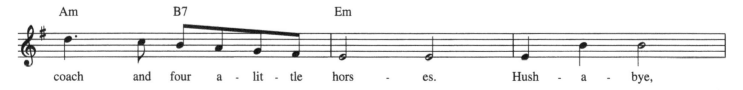

coach and four a - lit - tle hors - es. Hush - a - bye,

3rd time, To Coda **⊕ Coda**   *D.C. al Coda* **⊕ Coda**
(take repeats)

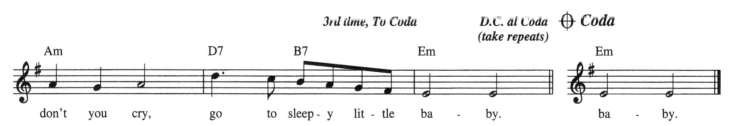

don't you cry, go to sleep - y lit - tle ba - by.   ba - by.

Additional Lyrics

2. Hush-a-bye, don't you cry,
   Go to sleepy, little baby.
   Way down yonder in the meadow
   Lies a poor little lambie.

3. The bees and the butterflies pecking out its eyes,
   The poor little thing cried, "Mammy."
   Hush-a-bye, don't you cry,
   Go to sleepy, little baby.

Animal Fair

Traditional

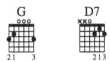

Strum Pattern: 8
Pick Pattern: 8

Lively

I went to the an - i - mal fair, _____ the birds and

beasts were there. _____ The big ba - boon, by the light of the

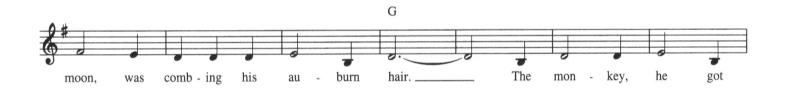

moon, was comb - ing his au - burn hair. _____ The mon - key, he got

drunk, _____ and sat on the el - e - phant's trunk. _____ The

el - e - phant sneezed, and fell on his knees, and what be -

came of the monk, the monk, the monk, the monk?

Annie Laurie

Strum Pattern: 2
Pick Pattern: 4

Verse
Moderately

1. Max - wel - ton's braes are bon - nie, where ear - ly fa's the dew. And it's there that An - nie Lau - rie gave me her prom - ise true. Gave me her prom - ise true, which ne'er for - got will be. And for bon - nie An - nie Lau - rie I'd lay me doon and dee. 2. Her dee.

2., 3. *See Additional Lyrics*

Chorus

Additional Lyrics

2. Her brow is like the snowdrift
   Her neck is like the swan.
   Her face it is the fairest
   That e'er the sun shone on.
   That e'er the sun shone on,
   An' dark blue is her e'e...

3. Like dew on the gowan lying
   Is the fa' o' her fairy feet;
   An' like the winds in summer sighing,
   Her voice is low an' sweet.
   Her voice is low an' sweet,
   An' she's a' the world to me.

Aura Lee

Music by George R. Poulton
Lyrics by W. W. Fosdick

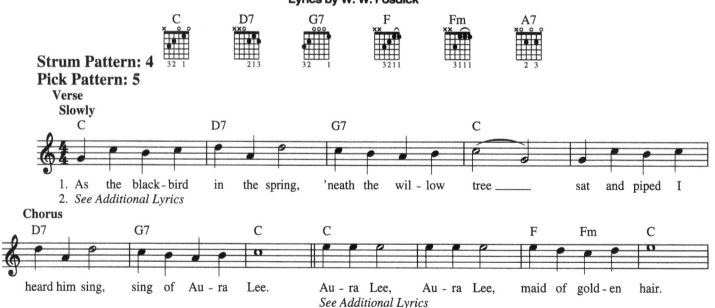

Strum Pattern: 4
Pick Pattern: 5

Verse
Slowly

1. As the black - bird in the spring, 'neath the wil - low tree sat and piped I

2. *See Additional Lyrics*

Chorus

heard him sing, sing of Au - ra Lee. Au - ra Lee, Au - ra Lee, maid of gold - en hair.

See Additional Lyrics

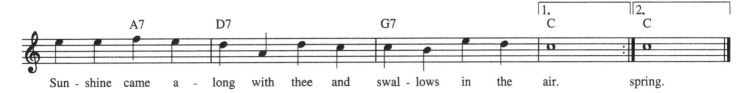

Sun - shine came a - long with thee and swal - lows in the air. spring.

Additional Lyrics

2. In thy blush the rose was born,
   Music when you spake.
   Though thine azure eyes the moon
   Sparkling seemed to break.

Chorus Aura Lee, Aura Lee, birds of crimson wing,
   Never song have sung to me as
   In that bright, sweet spring.

Billy Boy

Traditional

Strum Pattern: 10
Pick Pattern: 10

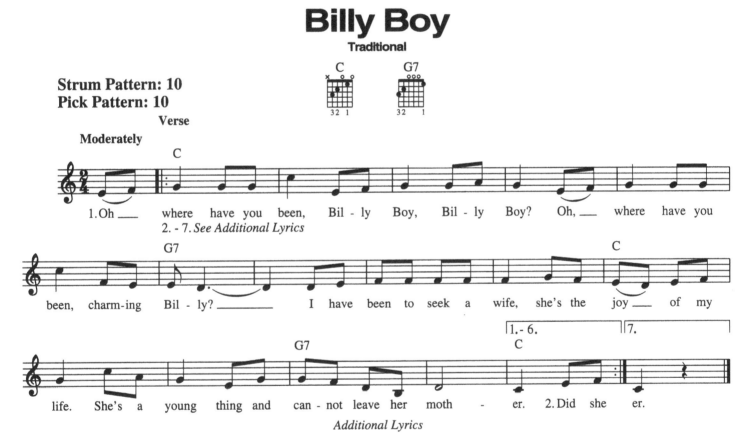

1. Oh __ where have you been, Bil - ly Boy, Bil - ly Boy? Oh, __ where have you
2. - 7. *See Additional Lyrics*

been, charm - ing Bil - ly? __ I have been to seek a wife, she's the joy __ of my

life. She's a young thing and can - not leave her moth - er. 2. Did she er.

Additional Lyrics

2. Did she bid you come in, Billy Boy, Billy Boy?
   Did she bid you come in charming Billy?
   Yes, she bade me to come in,
   Let me kiss her on the chin.
   She's a young thing and cannot leave her mother.

3. Did she set for you a chair, Billy Boy, Billy Boy?
   Did she set for you a chair, charming Billy?
   Yes, she set for me a chair
   And the bottom wasn't there.
   She's a young thing and cannot leave her mother.

4. Can she bake a cherry pie, Billy Boy, Billy Boy?
   Can she bake a cherry pie, charming Billy?
   She can bake a cherry pie
   Quick as a cat can wink her eye.
   She's a young thing and cannot leave her mother.

5. How old is she, Billy Boy, Billy Boy?
   How old is she, charming Billy?
   She's three times six and four times seven,
   Twenty-eight and eleven.
   She's a young thing and cannot leave her mother.

6. Can she sing a pretty song, Billy Boy, Billy Boy?
   Can she sing a pretty song, charming Billy?
   She can sing a pretty song
   But she gets the words all wrong.
   She's a young thing and cannot leave her mother.

7. Are her eyes very bright, Billy Boy, Billy Boy?
   Are her eyes very bright, charming Billy?
   Yes, her eyes are very bright
   But unfortunately lack sight,
   And she can't describe me to her mother.

Annabel Lee

Traditional

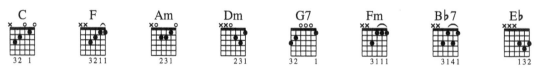

Strum Pattern: 7
Pick Pattern: 9

Verse

Additional Lyrics

2. For I was a child and she was a child,
   In this kingdom by the sea.
   But we loved with a love that was greater than love,
   So loved I and my Annabel Lee.
   With a love so strong that the angels watched,
   Even coveted her and me.
   With a love so strong that the angels watched,
   Even coveted her and me!

3. And this is the reason that long, long ago,
   In this kingdom by the sea,
   There arose a strong wind blowing out of a cloud,
   Chilled and killed my dear Annabel Lee.
   And her highborn kinsmen they quickly came,
   And they bore her away from me.
   And they sealed her remains in a sepulcher deep,
   In this kingdom by the sea!

4. But our love it was stronger by far than the love
   Of the ones who were older than we,
   Of the many far older and wiser than we,
   Of those older and wiser than we.
   Ah, but neither angel in sky above
   Nor the demons beneath the sea
   Could sever my soul from the soul of my love
   Of my beautiful Annabel Lee!

5. And the moon never beams without bringing me dreams
   In this kingdom by the sea.
   And the stars never ride but I feel the bright eyes
   Of the beautiful Annabel Lee.
   Thru the night I lie by my dearest one,
   By the side of my bride to be.
   Though she lies in her sepulcher silent and cold
   Oh, my beautiful Annabel Lee!

Beautiful Brown Eyes

Traditional

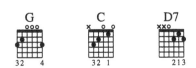

Strum Pattern: 7
Pick Pattern: 9

Chorus
Moderately

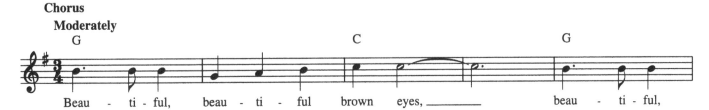

Beau - ti - ful, beau - ti - ful brown eyes, _____ beau - ti - ful,

beau - ti - ful brown eyes. _____ Beau - ti - ful, beau - ti - ful

To Coda ⊕

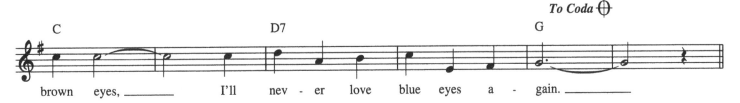

brown eyes, _____ I'll nev - er love blue eyes a - gain. _____

Verse

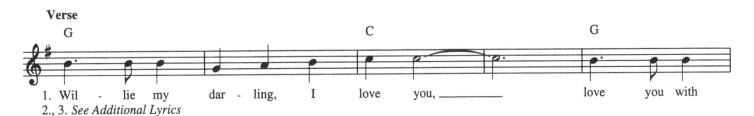

1. Wil - lie my dar - ling, I love you, _____ love you with
2., 3. *See Additional Lyrics*

all of my heart. To - mor - row we were to be mar - ried, _____

1., 2., 3.   *3rd time, D.C. al Coda*   ⊕ *Coda*

_____ but liq - uor has kept us a - part. _____

Additional Lyrics

2. I staggered into the barroom,
I fell down on the floor.
And the very last words that I uttered,
"I'll never get drunk any more."

3. Seven long years I've been married,
I wish I was single again.
A woman don't know half her troubles
Until she has married a man.

Banks of the Ohio

Traditional

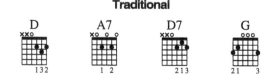

Strum Pattern: 3
Pick Pattern: 3

Moderately

I asked my love _____ to take a walk, _____ to take a walk, _____ just a lit - tle walk, _____ _____ down be - side, _____ where the wa - ters flow. _____ _____ Down by the banks _____ of the O - hi - o.

Black Is the Color of My True Love's Hair

Traditional

Strum Pattern: 2
Pick Pattern: 4

Verse

Freely

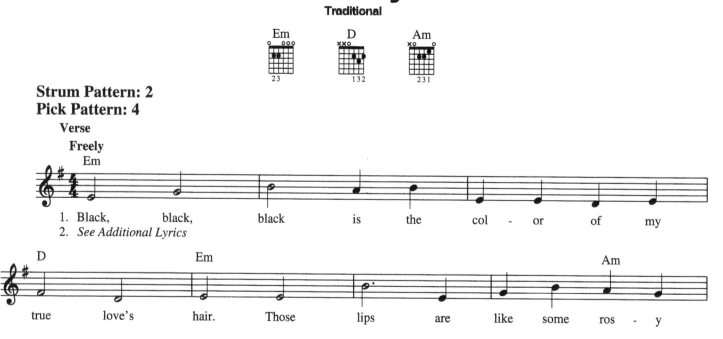

1. Black, black, black is the col - or of my
2. *See Additional Lyrics*

true love's hair. Those lips are like some ros - y

fair. The pur - est _____ eyes and the neat - est _____

hands, I love the grass where - on she stands. o - ver be.

Additional Lyrics

2. How I love my love and well she knows,
   I love the grass whereon she goes.
   When she on earth no more I see,
   My life will quickly over be.

Bury Me Not on the Lone Prairie

Words based on the poem "The Ocean Burial" by E.H. Chapin
Music by George N. Allen

Strum Pattern: 3
Pick Pattern: 1

1. Oh, bur - ry me not _____ on the lone prai - rie. _____
2. - 4. *See Additional Lyrics*

_____ These words came low _____ and so mourn - ful - ly, _____ from the pal - lid

lips _____ of a youth who lay, _____ on his dy ing bed _____

_____ at the close of day. _____ 2. Oh, bur - y me _____

Additional Lyrics

2. Oh, bury me not the lone prairie.
   Where the coyotes howl and the wind blows free;
   In a narrow grave just six by three.
   Oh, bury me not on the lone prairie.

3. "Oh, bury me not," and this voice failed there.
   But we took no heed of his dying prayer;
   In a narrow grave just six by three.
   We buried him there on the lone prairie.

4. Yes, we buried him there on the lone prairie.
   Where the owl all night hoots mournfully;
   And the blizzard beats and the wind blows free,
   O'er his lonely grave on the lone prairie.

The Big Rock Candy Mountain

Words, Music and Arrangement by Harry K. McClintock

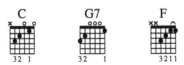

Strum Pattern: 3
Pick Pattern: 3

Moderately

On a sum-mer day in the month of May, a __ bur-ly bum came hik-ing. Down a

shad-y lane, thru the sug-ar cane he was look-ing for his lik-ing. As he

roamed a-long he sang a song of the land of milk and hon-ey. __ Where a

bum can stay for __ man-y a day and he won't need an-y mon-ey. Oh! the

Chorus

buzz-in' of the bees in the cig-ar-ette trees, near the so-da wa-ter foun-tain. At the

lem-on-ade springs where the blue-bird sings, in the Big Rock Can-dy Moun-tain.

The Blue Tail Fly
(Jimmy Crack Corn)

Words and Music by Daniel Decatur Emmett

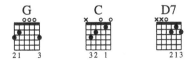

Strum Pattern: 3
Pick Pattern: 4

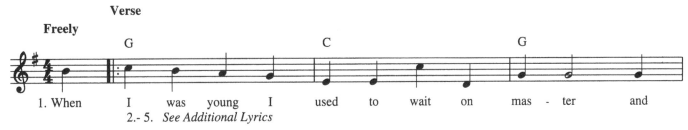

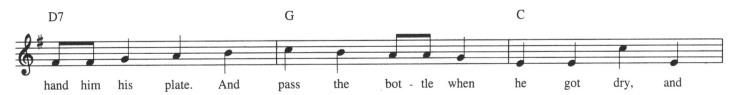

Additional Lyrics

2. And when he'd ride in the afternoon,
   I'd follow after with a hickory broom.
   The pony being very shy,
   When bitten by Blue Tail Fly!

3. One day while riding round the farm,
   The flies so numerous they did swarm.
   One chanced, to bite him on the thigh,
   The devil take the Blue Tail Fly!

4. The pony run, he jump, he kick,
   He threw my master in the ditch.
   He died and the jury wondered why,
   The verdict was the Blue Tail Fly!

5. They laid him under a 'simmon tree.
   His epitaph is there to see.
   "Beneath this stone Jim forced to lie,
   A victim of the Blue Tail Fly!"

Buffalo Gals
(Won't You Come out Tonight?)

Words and Music by Cool White (John Hodges)

Strum Pattern: 5
Pick Pattern: 1

Verse
Lively

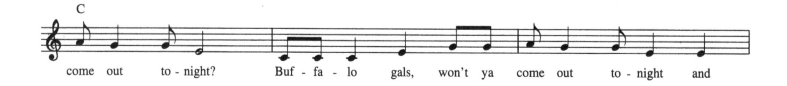

1. Buf - fa - lo gals, won't ya come out to - night, won't ya come out to - night, won't ya
2. *See Additional Lyrics*

come out to - night? Buf - fa - lo gals, won't ya come out to - night and

Chorus

dance by the light of the moon? I danced with a gal with a hole in her stock-ing and her

heel kept a - rock - in' and her toe kept a - knock-in'. I danced with a gal with a

hole in her stock-ing, and we danced by the light of the moon. moon.

Additional Lyrics

2. Yes, pretty boys, we'll come out tonight,
   We'll come out tonight, we'll come out tonight.
   Yes, pretty boys, we'll come out tonight
   And dance by the light of the moon.

Camptown Races

Music by Stephen Collins Foster

Strum Pattern: 3
Pick Pattern: 4

Verse
Fast

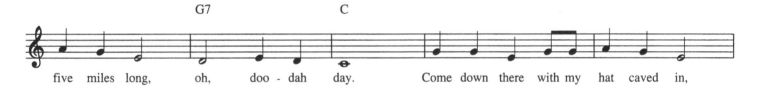

1. Camp-town la - dies sing this song, doo - dah, doo - dah. Camp-town race - track
2. - 4. *See Additional Lyrics*

five miles long, oh, doo - dah day. Come down there with my hat caved in,

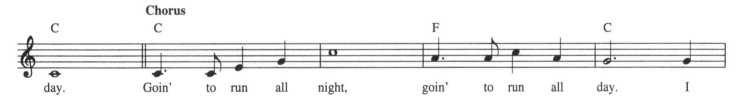

doo - dah, doo - dah. Go back home with my pock-et full of tin, oh, doo - dah

Chorus

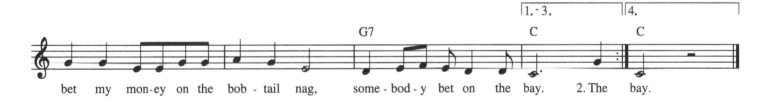

day. Goin' to run all night, goin' to run all day. I

bet my mon-ey on the bob - tail nag, some - bod - y bet on the bay. 2. The bay.

Additional Lyrics

2. The long-tail filly and the big black hoss, doodah, doodah.
   They fly the track and they both cut across, oh, doodah day.
   The blind hoss sticken in a big mud hole, doodah, doodah.
   Can't touch bottom with a ten-foot pole, oh, doodah day.

3. Old muley cow come onto the track, etc.
   The bobtail fling her over his back,
   Then fly along like a railroad car,
   Running a race with a shooting star,

4. See them flying on a ten-mile heat, etc.
   'Round the race track, then repeat,
   I win my money on the bobtail nag,
   I keep my money in an old towbag,

Careless Love

Anonymous

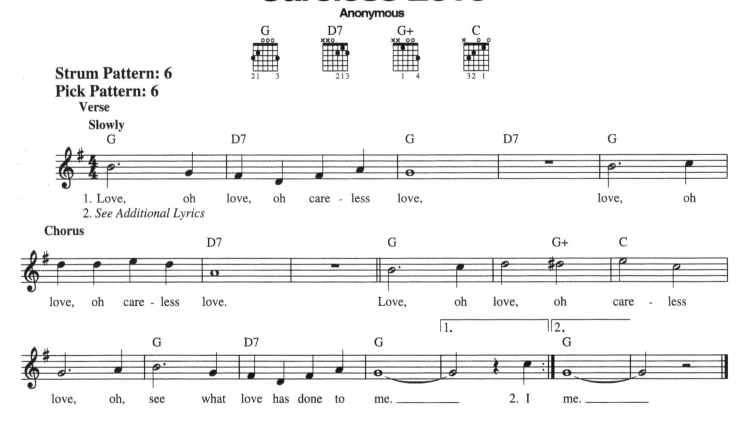

Strum Pattern: 6
Pick Pattern: 6

Verse
Slowly

1. Love, oh love, oh care-less love, love, oh
2. *See Additional Lyrics*

Chorus

love, oh care-less love. Love, oh love, oh care-less

love, oh, see what love has done to me. 2. I me.

Additional Lyrics

2. I cried last night and the night before.
   Tonight I'll cry, then cry no more.

Carry Me Back to Old Virginny

Traditional

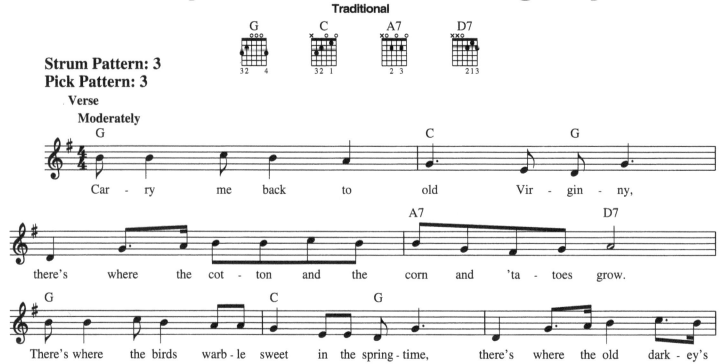

Strum Pattern: 3
Pick Pattern: 3

Verse
Moderately

Car - ry me back to old Vir - gin - ny,

there's where the cot - ton and the corn and 'ta - toes grow.

There's where the birds warb - le sweet in the spring - time, there's where the old dark - ey's

heart am longed to go. There's where I la - bored so ___ hard for old mas - sa,

day af - ter day in the fields of yel - low corn. No place on earth do I

love more sin - cere - ly than old Vir - gin - ny the ___ state where I was born.

Cindy

Traditional

Strum Pattern: 10
Pick Pattern: 10

Verse
Moderately

1. A sweet - er girl than Cin - dy, you nev - er, nev - er saw. Oh,
2. *See Additional Lyrics*

how I wish my love for her would be with - in the law. Get a - long

Chorus

home, Cin - dy, Cin - dy, get a - long home, Cin - dy, Cin - dy, get a - long

home, Cin - dy, Cin - dy, I'll mar - ry you some day. 2. I day.

Additional Lyrics

2. I wish I was an apple,
   A-hangin' from a tree.
   And ev'ry time that Cindy passed,
   She'd take a bite of me.

3. I wish I was a rich guy,
   With cash in several banks.
   I sure would buy nice things for her,
   To hear her whisper, "Thanks."

4. I wish that I were single,
   I wish that I were free.
   So I could change this dream of mine
   Into reality.

(Oh, My Darling) Clementine

Words and Music by Percy Montrose

Strum Pattern: 9
Pick Pattern: 7

1. In a cav-ern, in a can-yon, ex-ca-vat-ing for a mine, dwelt a
2. - 5. *See Additional Lyrics*

min-er for-ty nin-er and his daugh-ter, Clem-en-tine. Oh, my

Chorus

dar-ling, oh, my dar-ling, oh my dar-ling Clem-en-tine, you are

lost and gone for-ev-er, dread-ful sor-ry Clem-en-tine. 2. Light she tine.

Additional Lyrics

2. Light she was and like a fairy
   And her shoes were number nine,
   Herring boxes, without topses
   Sandals were for Clementine.

3. Drove she ducklings to the water
   Ev'ry mornig just at nine,
   Stubbed her toe upon a splinter
   Fell into the foaming brine.

4. Ruby lips above the water
   Blowing bubbles soft and fine,
   But alas I was no swimmer
   So I lost my Clemetine.

5. There's a churchyard on the hillside
   Where the flowers grow and twine,
   There grow roses 'mongst the posies
   Fertilized by Clementine.

Come All Ye Fair and Tender Maidens

Traditional

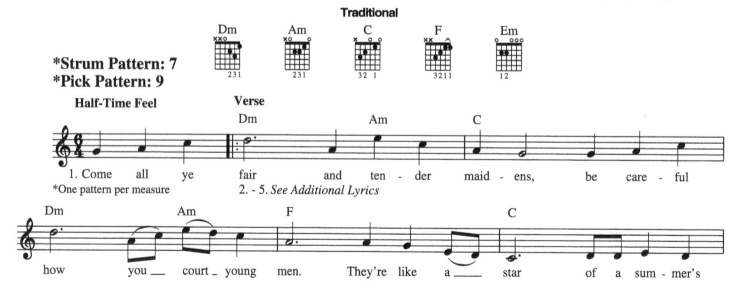

*Strum Pattern: 7
*Pick Pattern: 9

Half-Time Feel

Verse

1. Come all ye fair and ten-der maid-ens, be care-ful
*One pattern per measure   2. - 5. *See Additional Lyrics*

how you court young men. They're like a star of a sum-mer's

morn - ing, they'll first ap - pear and __ then they're gone. 2.They'll tell to pin.

Additional Lyrics

2. They'll tell to you some loving story,
   They'll declare to you their love is true.
   Straightway they'll go and court some other,
   And that's the love they have for you.

3. I wish I was some little sparrow,
   That I had wings, could fly so high.
   I'd fly away to my false true lover,
   And when he's talking, I'd be by.

4. But I am not a little sparrow,
   And neither have I wings to fly.
   I'll sit down here in grief and sorrow,
   To weep and pass my troubles by.

5. If I'd a-known before I courted,
   I never would have courted none.
   I'd have locked my heart in a box of golden,
   And pinned it up with a silver pin.

The Cruel War Is Raging

Traditional

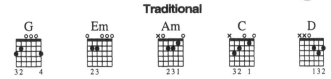

Strum Pattern: 2
Pick Pattern: 4

Moderately **Verse**

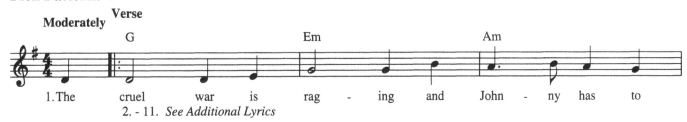

1.The cruel war is rag - ing and John - ny has to
2. - 11. *See Additional Lyrics*

fight, I want to be with him from morn - ing till night. 2. I'll yes.

Additional Lyrics

2. I'll go to your captain, get down upon my knees,
   Ten thousand gold guineas I'd give for your release.

3. Ten thousand gold guineas, it grieves my heart so,
   Won't you let me go with you? - Oh, no, my love, no.

4. Tomorrow is Sunday and Monday is the day
   Your captain calls for you, and you must obey.

5. Your captain calls for you, it grieves my heart so,
   Won't you let me go with you? - Oh, no, my love, no.

6. Your waist is too slender, your fingers are too small,
   Your cheeks are too rosy to face the cannonball.

7. Your cheeks are too rosy, it grieves my heart so,
   Won't you let me go with you? - Oh, no, my love, no.

8. Johnny, oh Johnny, I think you are unkind,
   I love you far better than all other mankind.

9. I love you far better than the tongue can express,
   Won't you let me go with you? - Oh, yes, my love, yes.

10. I'll pull back my hair, men's clothes I'll put on,
    I'll pass for your comrade as we march along.

11. I'll pass for your comrade and none will ever guess,
    Won't you let me go with you? - Yes, my love, yes.

Cotton-Eyed Joe

Traditional

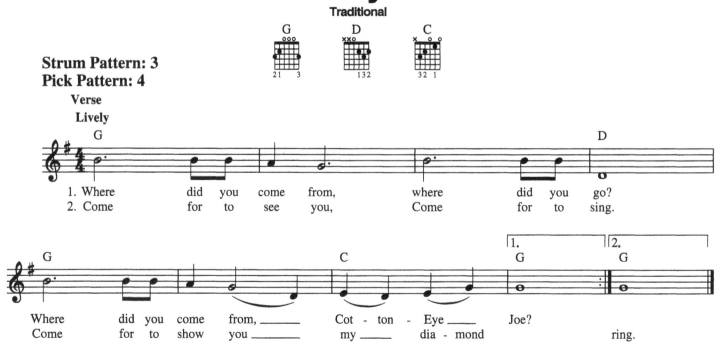

Strum Pattern: 3
Pick Pattern: 4

Verse
Lively

1. Where did you come from, where did you go?
2. Come for to see you, Come for to sing.

Where did you come from, _____ Cot - ton - Eye _____ Joe?
Come for to show you _____ my _____ dia - mond ring.

Deep River

Traditional

Strum Pattern: 4
Pick Pattern: 4

Chorus
Slowly

Deep _____ riv - er, my home is o - ver Jor - dan, _____ deep _____ riv - er, Lord, I want to cross o - ver in - to camp - ground. camp - ground. Oh, don't you want _____ to go _____ to that

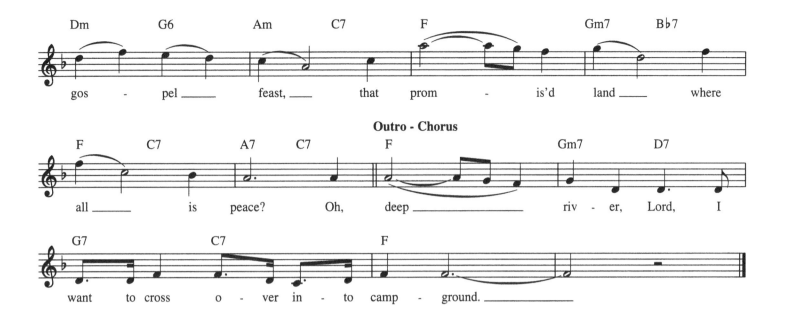

gos - pel ___ feast, ___ that prom - is'd land ___ where

Outro - Chorus

all ___ is peace? Oh, deep ___ riv - er, Lord, I

want to cross o - ver in - to camp - ground. ___

Down in the Valley

Traditional American Folksong

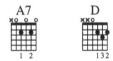

Strum Pattern: 7
Pick Pattern: 9

Verse

Moderately

1. Down in the val - ley, ___ val - ley so low, ___
2. *See Additional Lyrics*

hang your head o - ver, ___ hear the wind

blow. ___ 2. Ros - es love you.

Additional Lyrics

2. Roses love sunshine,
   Violets love dew,
   Angels in heaven
   Know I love you.

(I Wish I Was In) Dixie

Words and Music by Daniel Decatur Emmett

Strum Pattern: 3
Pick Pattern: 4

Verse
Brightly

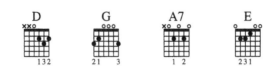

1. I ___ wish I was ___ in the land of cot - ton. Old times they're are

2. *See Additional Lyrics*

not for - got - ten. Look a - way! Look a - way! Look a - way! Dix - ie -

land. 2. In ___ land Oh I wish I was in Dix - ie. Hoo -

ray! Hoo - ray! In Dix - ie - land I'll take my stand to

live and die in Dix - ie. A - way, a - way, a - way down south in

Dix - ie. A - way, a - way, a - way down south in Dix - ie.

Additional Lyrics

2. In Dixieland where I was born,
   In early on one frosty mornin'.
   Look away! Look away!
   Look away! Dixieland.

The Drunken Sailor

Traditional

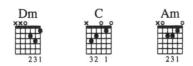

Strum Pattern: 3
Pick Pattern: 5

Verse
Lively

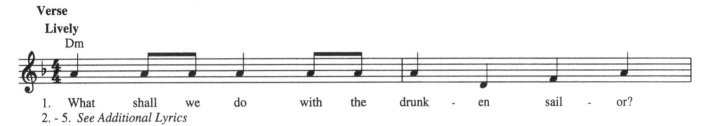

1. What shall we do with the drunk - en sail - or?
2. - 5. *See Additional Lyrics*

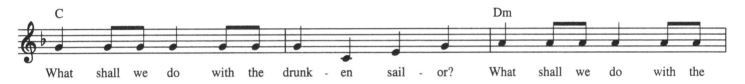

What shall we do with the drunk - en sail - or? What shall we do with the

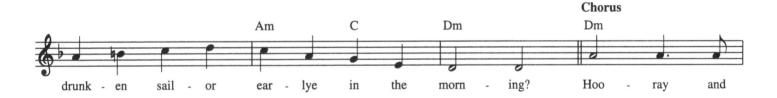

drunk - en sail - or ear - lye in the morn - ing? Hoo - ray and

Chorus

up she ris - es, hoo - ray and up she ris - es, hoo - ray and

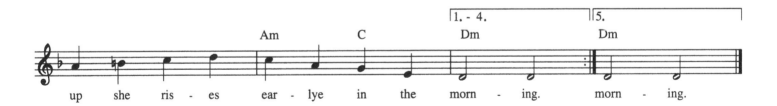

up she ris - es ear - lye in the morn - ing. morn - ing.

Additional Lyrics

2. Put him in the long boat till he's sober,
   Put him in the long boat till he's sober,
   Put him in the long boat till he's sober
   Earlye in the morning.

3. Pull out the plug and wet him all over,
   Pull out the plug and wet him all over,
   Pull out the plug and wet him all over
   Earlye in the morning.

4. Tie him to the top mast when she's under,
   Tie him to the top mast when she's under,
   Tie him to the top mast when she's under
   Earlye in the morning.

5. Put him in the scuppers with the hosepipe on him,
   Put him in the scuppers with the hosepipe on him,
   Put him in the scuppers with the hosepipe on him
   Earlye in the morning.

The Erie Canal

Traditional American Folksong

Strum Pattern: 1
Pick Pattern: 4

Verse
Moderately

1. I've got a mule, her name is Sal, fif - teen miles on the E - rie Can - al. __ She's a
2. *See Additional Lyrics*

good old work - er and a good old pal, fif - teen miles on the E - rie Can - al. __ We've

hauled some barg - es in our day, filled with lum - ber, coal and hay. And we know ev - 'ry

Chorus

inch of the way from Al - ba - ny __ to __ Buf - fa - lo. __ Low bridge ev - 'ry - bod - y down!

Low bridge, for we're go - ing thru a town; And you'll al - ways know your neigh - bor, you'll

al - ways know your pal, if you've ev - er nav - ig - at - ed on the E - rie Can - al. _ 2. We'd E - rie Can - al. __

Additional Lyrics

2. We'd better get along our way,
Fifteen miles on the Erie Canal.
'Cause you bet your life I never part with Sal,
Fifteen miles on the Erie Canal.
Get up there mule here comes a lock
We'll make Rome 'bout six o'-clock.
One more trip and back we'll go,
Right back home to Buffalo.

Foggy Foggy Dew

Traditional

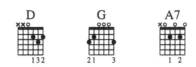

Strum Pattern: 3
Pick Pattern: 3

Verse

Moderately

1. When I was a bach-'lor I lived by my-self, I worked at the weav-er's
2., 3. *See Additional Lyrics*

trade. _____ And the on-ly, on-ly thing I did that was wrong was to

woo a fair young maid. I wooed her in the win-ter-time and

in the sum-mer, too. And the on-ly, on-ly thing I

did that was wrong was to keep her from the fog-gy, fog-gy dew. 2. One dew.

Additional Lyrics

2. One night she came to my bedside
   When I was fast asleep.
   She flung her arms around my neck
   And then began to weep.
   She wept, she cried, she tore her hair.
   Ah me, what could I do?
   So all night long I held her in my arms
   Just to keep her from the foggy, foggy dew.

3. Still I am a bach'lor, I live with my son,
   We work at the weavers trade.
   And ev'ry time I look into his eyes
   He reminds me of that fair young maid.
   He reminds me of the wintertime,
   And part of the summer, too.
   And of the many, many times I held her in my arms
   Just to keep her from the foggy, foggy dew.

Frankie and Johnny

Traditional

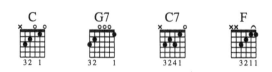

Strum Pattern: 3
Pick Pattern: 3

Verse
Moderately

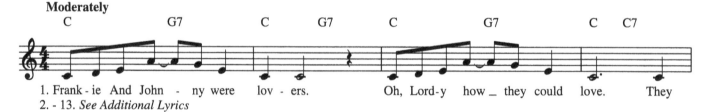

1. Frank-ie And John-ny were lov-ers. Oh, Lord-y how they could love. They
2. - 13. *See Additional Lyrics*

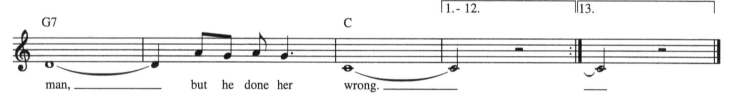

swore to be true to each oth-er just as true as the stars a-bove. He was her

man, but he done her wrong.

Additional Lyrics

2. Frankie she was a good woman
As everybody knows,
Spent a hundred dollars
Just to buy her man some clothes.
He was her man, but he was doing her wrong.

3. Frankie went down to the corner
Just for a bucket of beer,
Said, "Mr. bartender
Has my loving Johnny been here?
He was my man, but he's a-doing me wrong."

4. "Now I don't want to tell you no stories
And I don't want to tell you no lies.
I saw your man about an hour ago
With a gal named Nellie Bligh.
He was your man, but he's a-doing you wrong."

5. Frankie she went down to the hotel
Didn't go there for fun,
Underneath her kimona
She carried a forty-four gun.
He was her man, but he was doing her wrong.

6. Frankie looked over the transom
To see what she could spy.
There sat Johnny on the sofa
Just loving up Nellie Bligh.
He was her man, but he was doing her wrong.

7. Frankie got down from that high stool
She didn't want to see no more,
Rooty-toot-toot three times she shot
Right through that hardwood door.
He was her man, but he was doing her wrong.

8. Now the first time that Frankie shot Johnny
He let out an awful yell,
Second time she shot him
There was a new man's face in hell.
He was her man, but he was doing her wrong.

9. "Oh, roll me over easy,
Roll me over slow,
Roll me over on the right side
For the left side hurts me so."
He was her man, but he was doing her wrong.

10. Sixteen rubber-tired carriages,
Sixteen rubber-tired hacks,
They take poor Johnny to the graveyard
They ain't gonna bring him back.
He was her man, but he was doing her wrong.

11. Frankie looked out of the jailhouse
To see what she could see,
All she could hear was a two-string bow
Crying nearer my God to Thee.
He was her man, but he was doing her wrong.

12. Frankie said to the sheriff,
"What do you reckon they'll do?"
Sheriff he said, "Frankie,
"It's the electric chair for you."
He was her man, but he was doing her wrong.

13. This story has no moral,
This story has no end.
This story only goes to show
That there ain't no good in men!
He was her man, but he was doing her wrong.

Git Along, Little Dogies

Traditional

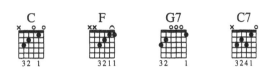

Strum Pattern: 7
Pick Pattern: 9

Verse
Moderately

1. As I was a-walk-in' one morn-ing for pleas-ure, I spied a cow-
2. - 7. *See Additional Lyrics*

punch-er a-stroll-in' a-long. His hat was thrown back and his spurs were a-jin-glin', and

Chorus

as he ap-proached he was sing-ing this song. Whoop-ee ti-yi-yo, git a-long lit-tle

do-gies, it's your ___ mis-for-tune, and none of my own. Whoop-ee ti-yi-yo, git a

long lit-tle do-gies, you know that Wy-o-ming will be your new home. 2. Ear-by.

Additional Lyrics

2. Early in the springtime we'll round up the dogies,
   Slap on their brands and bob off their tails.
   Round up our horses, load up the chuck wagon,
   Then throw those dogies upon the trail.

3. It's whooping and yelling and driving the dogies,
   Oh, how I wish you would go on.
   It's whooping and punching and go on, little dogies,
   For you know Wyoming will be your new home.

4. Some of the boys goes up the trail for pleasure,
   But that's where they git it most awfully wrong.
   For you haven't any idea the trouble they give us,
   When we go driving them dogies along.

5. When the night comes on and we hold them on the bed-ground,
   These little dogies that roll on so slow.
   Roll up the herd and cut out the strays,
   And roll the little dogies that never rolled before.

6. Your mother she was raised way down in Texas,
   Where the jimson weed and sandburs grow.
   Now we'll fill you up on prickly pear and cholla,
   Till you are ready for the trail to Idaho.

7. Oh, you'll be soup for Uncle Sam's Injuns,
   "It's beef, heap beef," I hear them cry.
   Git along, git along, git along little dogies,
   You're going to be beef steers by and by.

Give Me That Old Time Religion

Traditional

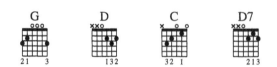

Strum Pattern: 3
Pick Pattern: 4

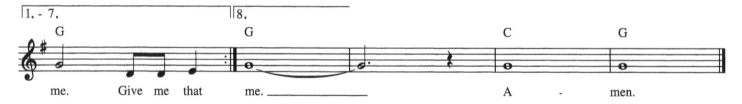

Additional Lyrics

2. Makes me love everybody,
   Makes me love everybody,
   Makes me love everybody,
   And it's good enough for me.

3. It has saved our fathers,
   It has saved our fathers,
   It has saved our fathers,
   And it's good enough for me.

4. It was good for the prophet Daniel,
   It was good for the prophet Daniel,
   It was good for the prophet Daniel,
   And it's good enough for me.

5. It was good for the Hebrew children,
   It was good for the Hebrew children,
   It was good for the Hebrew children,
   And it's good enough for me.

6. It was tried in the fiery furnace,
   It was tried in the fiery furnace,
   It was tried in the fiery furnace,
   And it's good enough for me.

7. It was good for Paul and Silas,
   It was good for Paul and Silas,
   It was good for Paul and Silas,
   And it's good enough for me.

8. It will do when I am dying,
   It will do when I am dying,
   It will do when I am dying,
   And it's good enough for me.

Goober Peas

Traditional

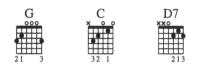

Strum Pattern: 3
Pick Pattern: 3

Verse
Moderately

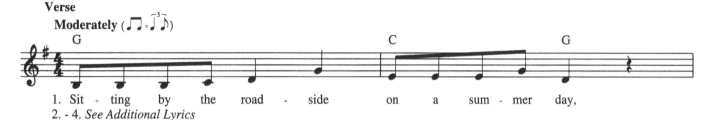

1. Sit - ting by the road - side on a sum - mer day,
2. - 4. *See Additional Lyrics*

chat - ting with my mess - mates, pass - ing time a - way. Ly - ing in the shad - ow

un - der - neath the trees, good - ness how de - li - cious, eat - ing Goo - ber Peas!

Chorus

Peas! Peas! Peas! Peas! Eat - ing Goo - ber Peas! Good - ness how de - li - cious,

eat - ing Goo - ber Peas! gob - ble Goo - ber Peas!

Additional Lyrics

2. When a horseman passes, the soldiers have a rule,
   To cry out at their loudest, "Mister, here's your mule!"
   But another pleasure enchantinger than these,
   Is wearing out your grinders, eating Goober Peas!

3. Just before the battle the gen'ral hears a row,
   He says, "The Yanks are coming, I hear their rifles now."
   He turns around in wonder, and what do you think he sees?
   The Georgia Militia eating Goober Peas!

4. I think my song has lasted almost long enough,
   The subject's interesting, but rhymes are mighty rough.
   I wish this war was over, when free from rags and fleas,
   We'd kiss our wives and sweethearts and gobble Goober Peas!

Good Night Ladies

Traditional

Goodbye, Old Paint

Traditional

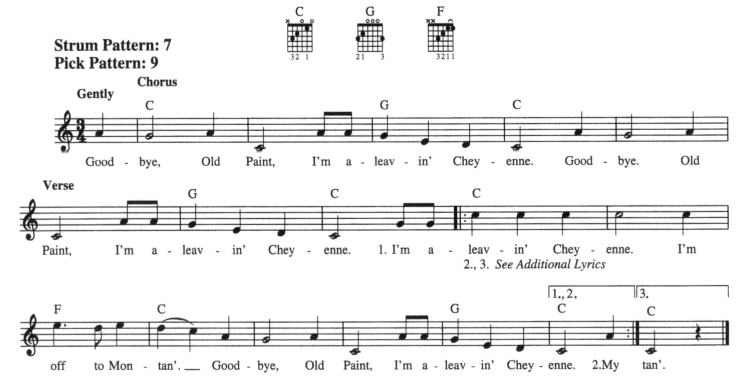

Additional Lyrics

2. My foot in the stirrup,
   My pony won't stand.
   Goodbye, Old Paint,
   I'm leavin' Cheyenne.

3. Old Paint's a good pony,
   He paces when he can.
   Goodbye little Annie,
   I'm off to Montan'.

Home on the Range

Traditional

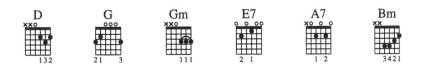

Strum Pattern: 7
Pick Pattern: 9

Verse
Slowly

Oh give me a home where the buf - fa - lo roam, where the

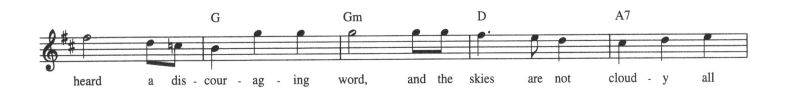

deer and the an - te - lope play. _____ Where sel - dom is

heard a dis - cour - ag - ing word, and the skies are not cloud - y all

Chorus

day. _____ Home, home on the range, _____ where the deer and the

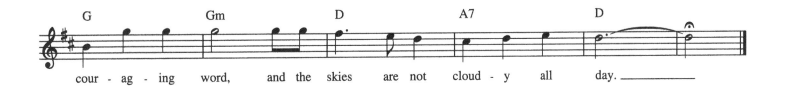

an - te - lope play. _____ Where sel - dom is heard a dis -

cour - ag - ing word, and the skies are not cloud - y all day. _____

He's Got the Whole World in His Hands

Traditional Spiritual

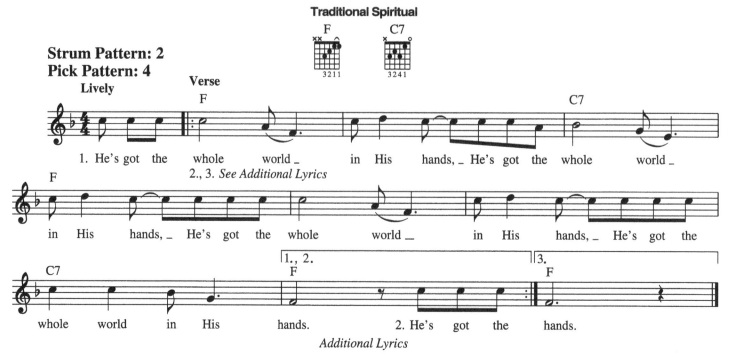

Strum Pattern: 2
Pick Pattern: 4

1. He's got the whole world _ in His hands, _ He's got the whole world _
in His hands, _ He's got the whole world _ in His hands, _ He's got the
whole world in His hands.

2. He's got the hands.

Additional Lyrics

2. He's got the wind and the rain
   In His hands,
   He's got the wind and the rain
   In His hands,
   He's got the wind and the rain
   In His hands,
   He's got the whole world in His hands.

3. He's got the wee small baby
   In His hands,
   And He's got all you lovers
   In His hands,
   Oh, He's got everybody
   In His hands,
   He's got the whole world in His hands.

House of the Rising Sun

Traditional

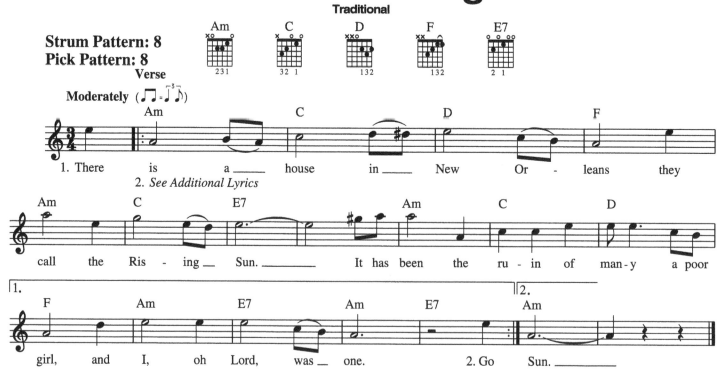

Strum Pattern: 8
Pick Pattern: 8

1. There is a _ house in _ New Or - leans they
call the Ris - ing _ Sun. _ It has been the ru - in of man - y a poor
girl, and I, oh Lord, was _ one.

2. Go Sun. _

Additional Lyrics

2. Go speak to my baby sister and say,
   "Don't do as I have done."
   Stay away from places like this one in New Orleans
   They call the Rising Sun.

How Can I Keep from Singing

Traditional

Strum Pattern: 8
Pick Pattern: 8

Verse
Moderately

1. My life flows on in end - less song a - bove earth's lam - en -
2., 3. *See Additional Lyrics*

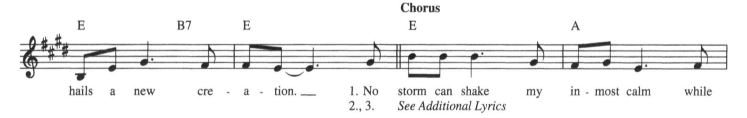

ta - tion. ___ I hear the real, through far off hymn that

Chorus

hails a new cre - a - tion. ___ 1. No storm can shake my in - most calm while
2., 3. *See Additional Lyrics*

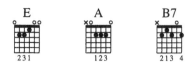

to that rock I'm cling - ing. ___ It sounds an ech - o ___

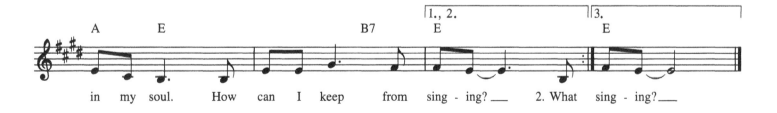

in my soul. How can I keep from sing - ing? ___ 2. What sing - ing? ___

Additional Lyrics

2. What though the tempest round me rears,
   I know the truth, it liveth.
   What though the darkness round me close,
   Songs in the nights it giveth.

Chorus 2. No storm can shake my inmost calm
   While to that rock I'm clinging.
   Since love is lord of Heaven and earth
   How can I keep from singing?

3. When tyrants tremble, sick with fear
   And hear their death knells ringing;
   When friends rejoice both far and near,
   How can I keep from singing?

Chorus 3. In prison cell and dungeon vile
   Our thoughts to them are winging.
   When friends by shame are undefiled
   How can I keep from singing?

Hush, Little Baby

Traditional

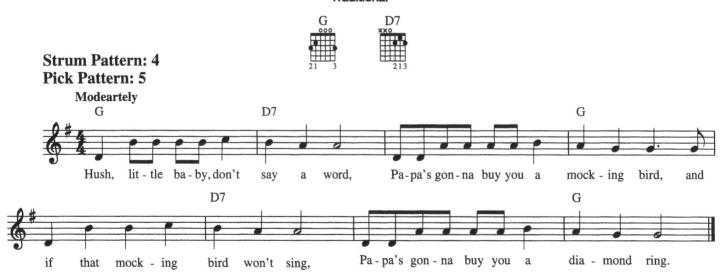

Strum Pattern: 4
Pick Pattern: 5

Modeartely

Hush, lit-tle ba-by, don't say a word, Pa-pa's gon-na buy you a mock-ing bird, and

if that mock-ing bird won't sing, Pa-pa's gon-na buy you a dia-mond ring.

I Gave My Love a Cherry

(The Riddle Song)

Traditional

Strum Pattern: 2
Pick Pattern: 2

Gently   **Verse**

1. I gave my love a cher-ry that had no
2., 3. *See Additional Lyrics*

stone. I gave my love a chick-en that had no

bone. I told my love a sto-ry that had no end. I

gave my love a ba-by with no cry-in'. How in'

Additional Lyrics

2. How can there be a cherry that has no stone?
   How can there be a chicken that has no bone?
   How can there be a story that has no end?
   How can there be a baby with no cryin'?

3. A cherry, when it's blooming, it has no stone.
   A chicken, when it's pipping, it has no bone.
   The story that I love, it has no end.
   A baby, when it's sleeping, has no cryin'.

John Henry

Traditional

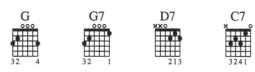

Strum Pattern: 3
Pick Pattern: 3

Verse

Moderately Fast

1. Well, __ ev - 'ry Mon - day __ morn - ing, when the
2. - 8. *See Additional Lyrics*

blue - birds be - gin to sing, you can see John

Hen - ry __ out on the line, you can hear John

Hen - ry's ham - mer ring, Lord, Lord, __ you can hear John

|1. - 7. Hen - ry's ham - mer ring. **|8.** 2. When __ man."

Additional Lyrics

2. When John Henry was a little baby,
   A-sitting on his papa's knee,
   He picked up a hammer and a little piece of steel,
   Said, "Hammer's gonna be the death of me, Lord, Lord,
   Hammer's gonna be the death of me."

3. Well, the Captain said to John Henry,
   "Gonna bring me a steam drill 'round,
   Gonna bring me a steam drill out on the Job,
   Gonna whip that steel on down, Lord, Lord,
   Gonna whip that steel on down."

4. John Henry said to his captain,
   "A man ain't nothin' but a man,
   And before I let that steam drill beat me down,
   I'll die with my hammer in my hand, Lord, Lord,
   I'll die with my hammer in my hand."

5. John Henry said to his shaker,
   "Shaker, why don't you pray?
   'Cause if I miss this little piece of steel,
   Tomorrow be your buryin' day, Lord, Lord,
   Tomorrow be your buryin' day."

6. John Henry was drivin' on the mountain
   And his hammer was flashing fire.
   And the last words I heard the poor boy say,
   "Gimme a cool drink of water 'fore I die, Lord, Lord,
   Gimme a cool drink of water 'fore I die."

7. John Henry, he drove fifteen feet,
   The steam drill made only nine,
   But he hammered so hard that he broke his poor heart,
   And he laid down his hammer and he died, Lord, Lord,
   And he laid down his hammer and he died.

8. They took John Henry to the graveyard
   And buried him in the sand
   And every locomotive comes a-roaring by says,
   "There lies a steel driving man, Lord, Lord,
   There lies a steel driving man."

I've Been Working on the Railroad

Traditional American Folksong

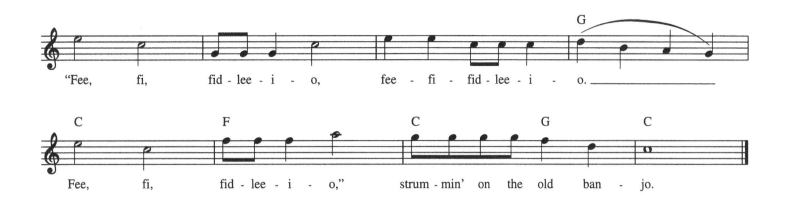

"Fee, fi, fid - lee - i - o, fee - fi - fid - lee - i - o. _____

Fee, fi, fid - lee - i - o," strum - min' on the old ban - jo.

Jacob's Ladder

Traditional Spiritual

Strum Pattern: 7
Pick Pattern: 9

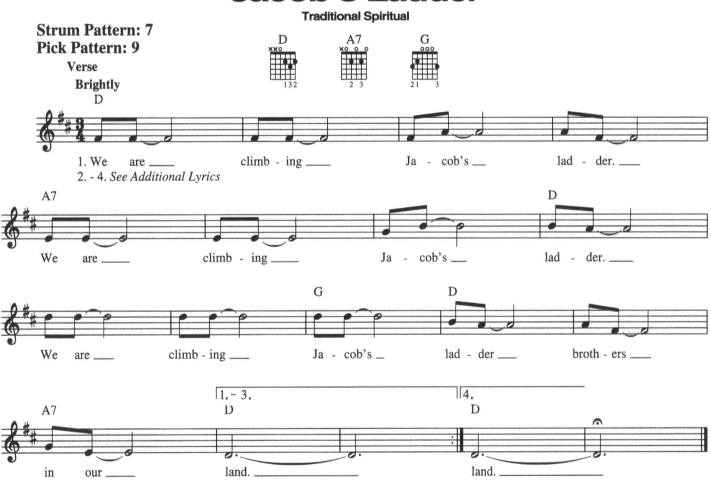

Verse
Brightly

1. We are ____ climb - ing ____ Ja - cob's ____ lad - der.
2. - 4. *See Additional Lyrics*

We are ____ climb - ing ____ Ja - cob's ____ lad - der.

We are ____ climb - ing ____ Ja - cob's ____ lad - der ____ broth - ers ____

in our ____ land. _____ land. _____

Additional Lyrics

2. Every rung goes higher, higher,
   Every rung goes higher, higher,
   Every rung goes higher, higher,
   Brothers in our land.

3. Every new man makes us stronger,
   Every new man makes us stronger,
   Every new man makes us stronger,
   Brothers in our land.

4. We have worked in dark and danger,
   We have worked in dark and danger,
   We have worked in dark and danger,
   Brothers in our land.

Little Brown Jug

Words and Music by Joseph E. Winner

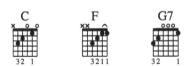

Strum Pattern: 3
Pick Pattern: 4

Verse

Gaily

1. My wife and I lived all a-lone in a lit-tle log hut we
2. *See Additional Lyrics*

called our own. She loved gin and I loved rum, I tell you what, we'd

Chorus

lots of fun! Ha, ha, ha, you and me, lit-tle brown jug, don't I love thee!

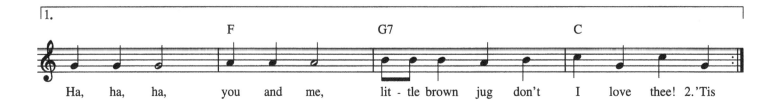

1.

Ha, ha, ha, you and me, lit-tle brown jug don't I love thee! 2.'Tis

2.

Ha, ha, ha, you and me, lit-tle brown jug don't I love thee!

Additional Lyrics

2. 'Tis you who makes my friends my foes,
   'Tis you who makes me wear old clothes.
   Here you are so near my nose,
   So tip her up and down she goes!

Long, Long Ago

by Thomas Bayly

Strum Pattern: 3
Pick Pattern: 3

Verse
Moderately

1.Tell me the tales that to me were so dear, long, long, a - go,
2., 3. *See Additional Lyrics*

long, long a - go. Sing me the songs I de - light - ed to hear,

long, long a - go, long a - go. Now you are come, all my grief is re - moved,

let me for - get that so long you have rov'd. Let me be - lieve that you

love as you loved, long, long a - go, long a - go. go.

Additional Lyrics

2. Do you remember the path where we met,
Long, long ago, long, long ago?
Ah yes, you told me you ne'er would forget,
Long, long ago, long ago.
Then, to all others, my smile you preferred,
Love, when you spoke, gave a charm to each word.
Still my heart treasures the praises I heard,
Long, long ago, long ago.

3. Tho' by your kindness my fond hopes were raised,
Long, long ago, long, long ago.
You, by more eloquent lips have been praised,
Long, long ago, long ago.
But by long absence your truth has been tried,
Still, to your accents, I listen with pride.
Blest as I was when I sat by your side,
Long, long ago, long ago.

My Old Kentucky Home

Words and Music by Stephen Collins Foster

Strum Pattern: 5
Pick Pattern: 5

Additional Lyrics

2. The young folks roll on the little cabin floor
   All merry, all happy and bright.
   By'n by hard times comes a-knocking at the door,
   Then my old Kentucky home, good night.

3. They hunt no more for the possum and the coon
   On meadow, the hill and the shore.
   They sing no more by the glimmer of the moon
   On the bench by that old cabin door.

4. The day goes by like a shadow o'er the heart,
   With sorrow where all was delight.
   The time has come when the good folks have to part,
   Then my old Kentucky home, good night.

5. The head must bow and the back will have to bend
   Wherever the poor folks may go.
   A few more days and the trouble will end
   In the field where the sugarcanes may grow.

6. A few more days for to tote the weary load.
   No matter, 'twill never by light.
   A few more days till we totter on the road,
   Then my old Kentucky home, good night.

Oh! Susanna

Words and Music by Stephen Collins Foster

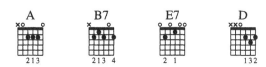

Strum Pattern: 3
Pick Pattern: 4

Additional Lyrics

2. It rained all night the day I left,
   The weather it was dry.
   The sun so hot I froze to death,
   Susanna don't you cry.

3. I had a dream the other night
   When everything was still.
   I thought I saw Susanna
   A-coming down the hill.

4. The buckwheat cake was in her mouth
   The tear was in her eye.
   Say I, "I'm coming from the South,
   Susanna, don't you cry."

The Lonesome Road

Traditional Black American Spiritual

Strum Pattern: 3
Pick Pattern: 4

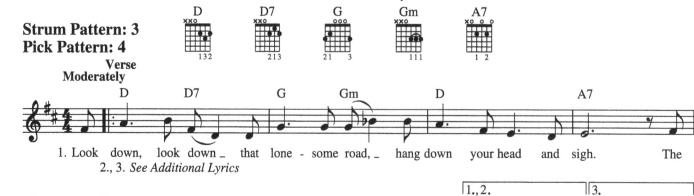

Verse
Moderately

1. Look down, look down __ that lone - some road, __ hang down your head and sigh. The

best of friends __ must part some day, __ and why not you and I? 2. True tongue.

Additional Lyrics

2. True love, true love, what have I done,
That you should treat me so?
You caused me to talk and to walk with you
Like I never done before.

3. I wish to God that I had died,
Had died 'fore I was born.
Before I seen your smilin' face,
And heard your lyin' tongue.

The Old Chisholm Trail

Traditional American Cowboy Song

Strum Pattern: 3
Pick Pattern: 3

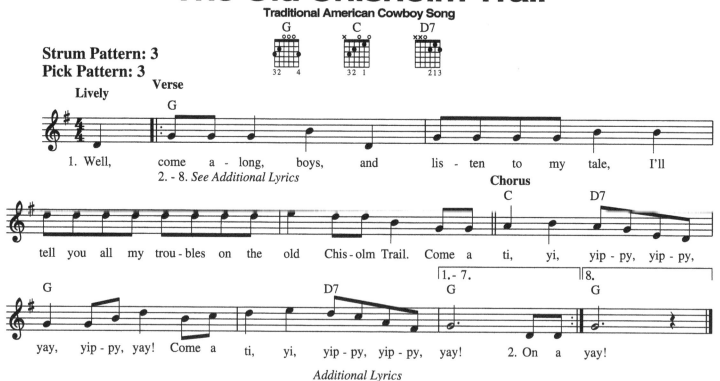

Lively   Verse

1. Well, come a - long, boys, and lis - ten to my tale, I'll

Chorus

tell you all my trou - bles on the old Chis - olm Trail. Come a ti, yi, yip - py, yip - py,

yay, yip - py, yay! Come a ti, yi, yip - py, yip - py, yay! 2. On a yay!

Additional Lyrics

2. On a ten dollar horse and a forty dollar saddle,
   I started out a-pinchin' those long-horned cattle.

3. I'm up in the morning before daylight,
   And before I gets to sleepin' the old moon's shining bright.

4. Oh, it's bacon and beans almost every single day,
   And I'd sooner be a-eatin' prairie hay.

5. I went to the boss for to draw my roll,
   He had it figured out I was nine dollars in the hole.

6. So I went up to the boss and said I won't take that,
   And I slapped him in the face with my old slouch hat.

7. I'll sell my outfit just as soon as I can,
   'Cause I ain't punchin' cattle for no mean boss man.

8. With my knees in the saddle and my seat in the sky,
   I'll quit punchin' cattle in the sweet by and by.

Old Folks At Home

Words and Music by Stephen Collins Foster

Strum Pattern: 2
Pick Pattern: 4

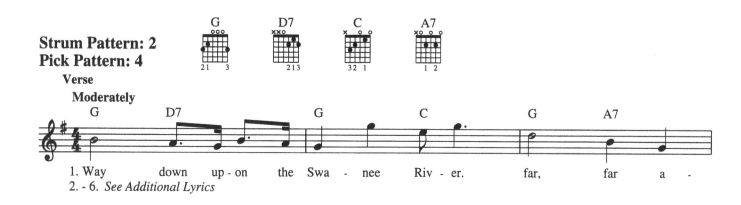

Verse
Moderately

1. Way down up - on the Swa - nee Riv - er, far, far a -
2. - 6. *See Additional Lyrics*

way. There's where my heart is turn - ing ev - er, there's where the old folks

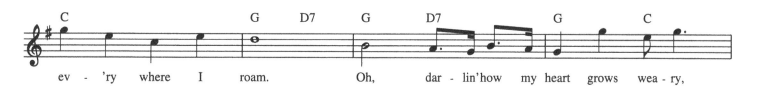

1., 3., 5. **2., 4., 6.** **Chorus**

stay. home. All the world is sad and drear - y

ev - 'ry where I roam. Oh, dar - lin' how my heart grows wea - ry,

last time, to Coda ⊕   *D.C. al Coda (take repeats)*   ⊕ *Coda*

far from the old folks at home.   home.

Additional Lyrics

2. All up and down the whole creation,
   Sadly I roam.
   Still longing for the old plantation,
   And for the old folks at home.

3. All 'round the little farm I wandered
   When I was young,
   Then many happy days I squandered,
   Many the songs I sung.

4. When I was playing with my brother,
   Happy was I.
   Oh, take me to my kind old mother,
   There let me live and die.

5. One little nut among the bushes,
   Happy was I.
   Still sadly to my mem'ry rushes,
   No matter where I rove.

6. When will I see the bees a-humming,
   All 'roun' the comb?
   When will I hear the banjo strumming,
   Down in my good old home?

Old Joe Clark

Traditional

Strum Pattern: 10
Pick Pattern: 10

Verse
Lively

1. Old Joe Clark, he had a house, six-teen sto-ries high. Ev-'ry sto-ry
2. - 4. *See Additional Lyrics*

Chorus

in the house smelled like ap-ple pie. 'Round and 'round, old Joe Clark,

'round and 'round, I says. 'Round and 'round, old Joe Clark, dance your cares a-way. way!

Additional Lyrics

2. I went up to Joe's new house,
Stepped right in the door.
Joe was sleepin' on a feather bed,
I had to sleep on the floor.

3. Old Joe Clark he had a dog,
Dumb as he could be.
Barked a ladybug up a stump,
A pig up a hollow tree.

4. Old Joe Clark had a mean old cat,
Never did sing or pray.
Stuck her head in the milking pail,
Washed her sins away!

On Top of Old Smoky

Traditional

Strum Pattern: 8
Pick Pattern: 8

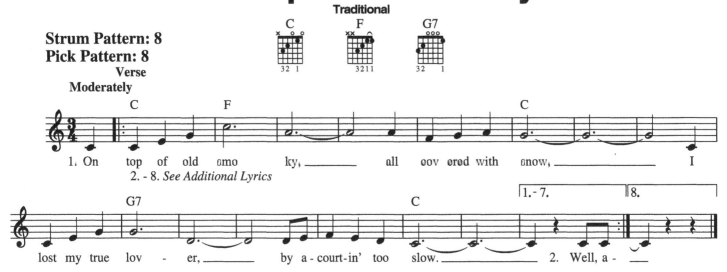

Verse
Moderately

1. On top of old smo ky, _____ all cov ered with snow, _____ I
2. - 8. *See Additional Lyrics*

lost my true lov er, _____ by a-court-in' too slow. _____ 2. Well, a- _____

Additional Lyrics

2. Well, a-courting's a pleasure,
And parting is grief.
But a false-hearted lover
Is worse than a thief.

3. A thief he will rob you
And take all you have,
But a false-hearted lover
Will send you to your grave.

4. And the grave will decay you
And turn you to dust.
And where is the young man
A poor girl can trust?

5. They'll hug and kiss you
And tell you more lies
Than the cross-ties on the railroad,
Or the stars in the skies.

6. They'll tell you they love you,
Just to give your heart ease.
But the minute your back's turned,
They'll court whom they please.

7. So come all you young maidens
And listen to me.
Never place your affection
On a green willow tree.

8. For the leaves they will wither
And the roots they will die.
And your true love will leave you,
And you'll never know why.

The Red River Valley

Traditional American Cowboy Song

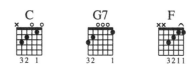

Strum Pattern: 4
Pick Pattern: 5

Verse

Moderately

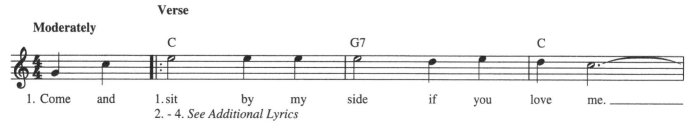

1. Come and 1. sit by my side if you love me. ___
2. - 4. *See Additional Lyrics*

___ Do not has - ten to bid me a -

dieu. ___ But re - mem - ber the red riv - er

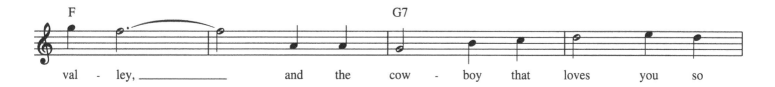

val - ley, ___ and the cow - boy that loves you so

true. ___ 2. Won't you ___

Additional Lyrics

2. Won't you think of this valley you're leaving?
   Oh, how lonely, how sad it will be.
   Oh, think of the fond heart you're breaking.
   And the grief you are causing me.

3. From this valley they say your are going.
   When you may your darling go, too?
   Would you leave her behind unprotected,
   When she loves no other but you?

4. I have promised you, darling, that never
   Will a word from my lips cause you pain.
   And my life, it will be yours forever,
   If you only will love me again.

Rock Island Line

Traditonal

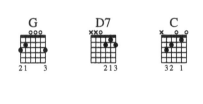

Strum Pattern: 3
Pick Pattern: 3

I say the Rock Is - land Line ___ is a migh - ty good road. ___ I say the

Rock Is - land Line ___ is the road to ride. ___ Oh, the Rock Is - land Line ___ is a

migh - ty good road. ___ If you ev - er want to ride it, got to ride it like you're

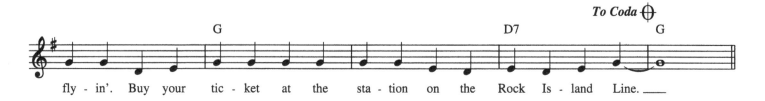

fly - in'. Buy your tic - ket at the sta - tion on the Rock Is - land Line. ___

Verse

1.A, B, C, dou - ble X, Y, Z, cat's in the cup - board, but
2., 3. *See Additional Lyrics*

3rd time, D.S. al Coda   ⊕ **Coda**

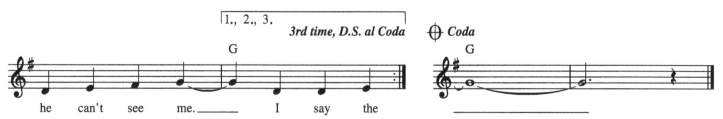

he can't see me. _____ I say the   _____

Additional Lyrics

2. Now Jesus died to save our sins,
   Glory be to God, we're going to need Him again.

3. I may be right and I may be wrong,
   I know you're gonna miss me when I am gone.

She'll Be Comin' 'Round the Mountain

Traditional

Strum Pattern: 2
Pick Pattern: 4

Verse

Fast

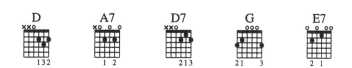

1. She'll be com - in' 'round the moun - tain when she comes.
2. - 4. *See Additional Lyrics*

She'll be com - in' round the moun - tain when she comes.

She'll be com - in' 'round the moun - tain, she'll be

com - in' 'round the moun - tain, she'll be com - in' 'round the

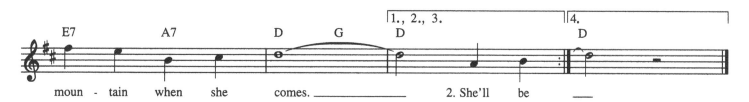

moun - tain when she comes. _____ 2. She'll be ___

Additional Lyrics

2. She'll be drivin' six white horses when she comes,
   She'll be drivin' six white horses when she comes.
   She'll be drivin' six white horses,
   She'll be drivin' six white horses,
   She'll be drivin' six white horses when she comes.

3. Oh, we'll all go out to meet her when she comes.
   Oh, we'll all go out to meet her when she comes.
   Oh, we'll all go out to meet her,
   Oh, we'll all go out to meet her,
   Yes, we'll all go out to meet her when she comes.

4. She'll be wearin' a blue bonnet when she comes.
   She'll be wearin' a blue bonnet when she comes.
   She'll be wearin' a blue bonnet,
   She'll be wearin' a blue bonnet,
   She'll be wearin' a blue bonnet when she comes.

Once I Had a Sweetheart

Traditional

Strum Pattern: 7
Pick Pattern: 9

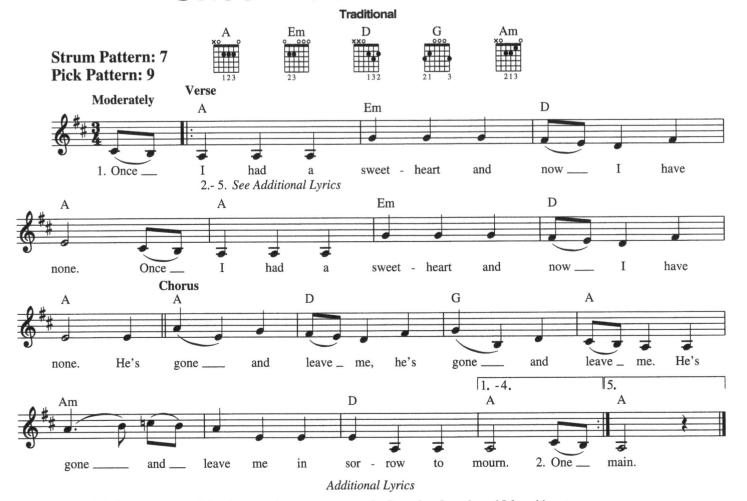

1. Once — I had a sweet-heart and now — I have
2.- 5. *See Additional Lyrics*

none. Once — I had a sweet-heart and now — I have

none. He's gone — and leave — me, he's gone — and leave — me. He's

gone — and — leave me in sor-row to mourn. 2. One — main.

Additional Lyrics

2. One night in sweet sorrow I lay down to sleep,
   My own fairest jewel sat smiling at me.

3. But when I awakened I found it not so,
   My eyes like some fountains with tears overflow.

4. My Billy is married or otherwise dead,
   His bunch of blue ribbons I'll wear 'round my head.

5. I'll travel through England, through France and through Spain,
   My life I will venture on the watery main.

Shenandoah

Traditional

Strum Pattern: 1
Pick Pattern: 2

O Shen-an-doah, — I love to see you. A-

way, — you roll-ing riv-er. O Shen-an-doah, — I long to see you. A-

way, — I'm bond a-way — a-cross the wide — Mis-sour-i.

Simple Gifts

Traditional

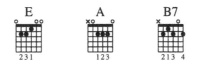

E   A   B7

Strum Pattern: 3
Pick Pattern: 3

Verse
Moderately

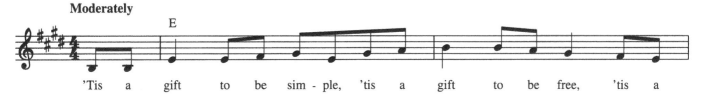

'Tis a gift to be sim - ple, 'tis a gift to be free, 'tis a

gift to come down where you ought to be. And

when we find our-selves in the place just right, 'twill be in the val - ley of

love and de - light. When true sim - plic - i - ty is gained, to

bow and to bend we ___ won't be a - shamed. To turn, turn will

be our de - light till by turn - ing and turn - ing we come out right.

Sometimes I Feel Like a Motherless Child

Traditional Spiritual

Strum Pattern: 10
Pick Pattern: 10

Verse
Slowly

1. Some-times I feel like a moth-er-less child. ____ Some-times I
2. *See Additional Lyrics*

feel like a moth-er-less child. ____ Some-times I feel like a

moth-er-less child, ____ a long way ____ from home, ____

____ a long ways ____ from home. _____

Additional Lyrics

2. Sometimes I feel like I'm almost gone.
   Sometimes I feel like I'm almost gone.
   Sometimes I feel like I'm almost gone,
   A long way from home,
   A long ways from home.

Streets of Laredo

Traditional

Strum Pattern: 8
Pick Pattern: 8

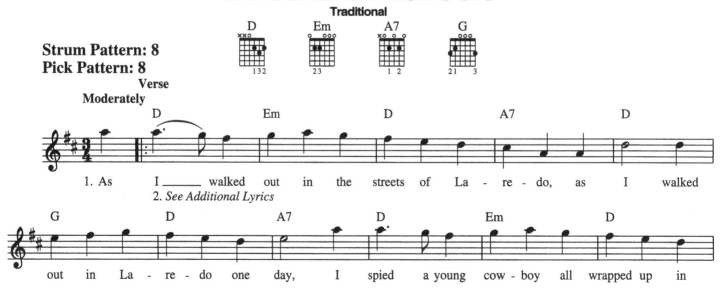

Verse
Moderately

1. As I ____ walked out in the streets of La-re-do, as I walked
2. *See Additional Lyrics*

out in La-re-do one day, I spied a young cow-boy all wrapped up in

lin - en, wrapped in white lin - en as cold as the day. 2. "I die."

Additional Lyrics

2. "I see by your outfit that you are a cowboy."
   These words, he did say as I proudly stepped by.
   "Come sit down beside me and hear my sad story.
   Got shot in the breast and I know I must die."

Steal Away

Traditional

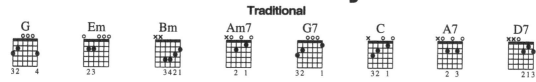

Strum Pattern: 4
Pick Pattern: 4

Chorus
Moderately

Steal a - way, steal a - way, steal a - way to Je - sus. Steal a - way,

steal a - way home. I ain't got long to stay here. 1. My Lord He

2., 3. *See Additional Lyrics*

calls me, He calls me by the thun - der, the trum - pet sounds with -

in ___ my soul. I ain't got long to stay here. stay here.

Additional Lyrics

2. Green trees a-bending,
   Poor sinners stand a-trembling,
   The trumpet sounds within my soul.
   I ain't got long to stay here.

3. My Lord He calls me,
   He calls me by the lightning,
   The trumpet sounds within my soul.
   I ain't got long to stay here.

Swing Low, Sweet Chariot

American Spiritual

This Little Light of Mine

Traditional

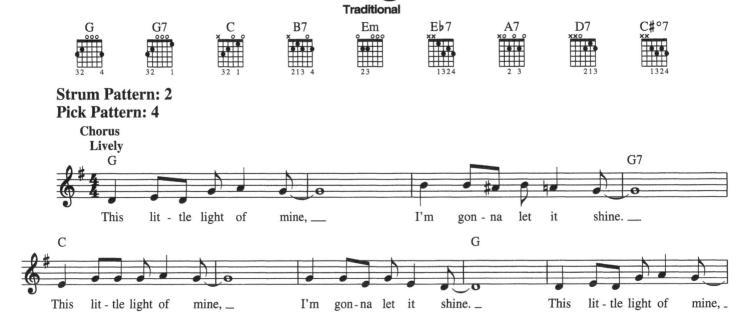

I'm gon-na let it shine. — Ev-'ry day, ev-'ry day, ev-'ry

To Coda ⊕

day, ev-'ry day, — gon-na let my lit-tle light shine. ——— On

Verse

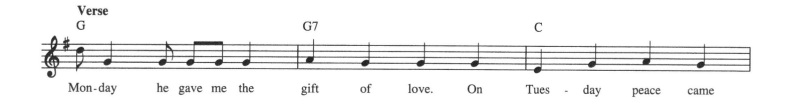

Mon-day he gave me the gift of love. On Tues-day peace came

from a - bove. On Wednes-day told me to have more faith. On

Thurs-day gave me a lit-tle more grace. On Fri - day told me to

watch and pray. On Sat-ur-day told mc just what to say. On

D.C. al Coda

Sun - day gave me the pow-er di - vine, just to let my lit-tle light shine. Oh,

⊕ *Coda*

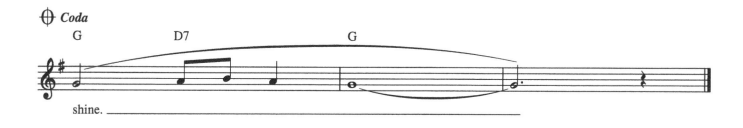

shine. ————————————

Sweet Betsy from Pike

Traditional

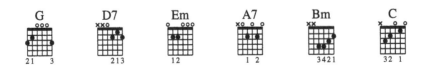

Strum Pattern: 7
Pick Pattern: 9

Verse

Brightly

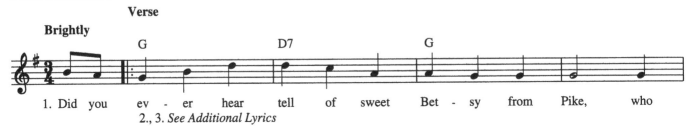

1. Did you ev - er hear tell of sweet Bet - sy from Pike, who
2., 3. *See Additional Lyrics*

crossed the wide prai - ries with her lov - er Ike? With two yoke of

ox - en and one spot - ted hog, a ___ tall shag - hai roost - er, an

old yel - low dog. Sing, ___ "Too - ral - i, oo - ral - i, oo - ral - i - ay."

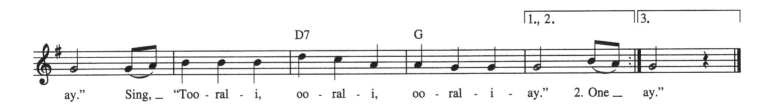

ay." Sing, ___ "Too - ral - i, oo - ral - i, oo - ral - i - ay." 2. One ___ ay."

Additional Lyrics

2. One evening quite early the camped on the Platte,
   'Twas near by the road on a green shady flat
   Where Betsy, quite tired, lay down to repose
   While with wonder Ike gazed on his Pike County rose.

3. They stopped at Salt Lake to inquire the way,
   Where Brigham declared that sweet Bets should stay.
   But Betsy got frightened and ran like a deer,
   While Brigham stood pawing the ground like a steer.

Take This Hammer

Traditional

Strum Pattern: 3
Pick Pattern: 4

Moderately   **Verse**

1. Take this ham-mer, _____ car-ry it to the cap - tain. _____ Take this ham-mer,

2. - 5. *See Additional Lyrics*

_____ car-ry it to the cap - tain. _____ Take this ham - mer, _____ car - ry it to the cap - tain, _____

_____ tell him I'm gone, _____ tell him I'm gone. _____ If he leg. _____

Additional Lyrics

2. If he asks you, was I laughin',
If he asks you, was I laughin',
If he asks you, was I laughin',
Tell him I was cryin', tell him I was cryin'.

3. If he asks you, was I runnin',
If he asks you, was I runnin',
If he asks you, was I runnin',
Thell him I was flyin', tell him I was flyin'.

4. I don't want no cornbread and molasses,
I don't want no cornbread and molasses,
I don't want no cornbread and molasses,
They hurt my pride, they hurt my pride.

5. I don't want no cold iron shacles,
I don't want no cold iron shacles,
I don't want no cold iron shacles,
Around my leg, around me leg.

The Wabash Cannon Ball

Traditional

Strum Pattern: 4
Pick Pattern: 5

Verse
Moderately

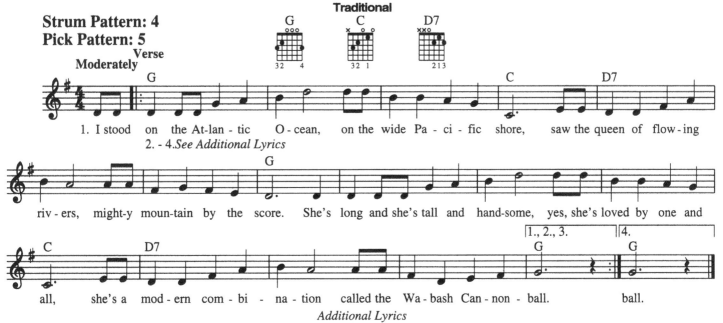

1. I stood on the At-lan - tic O - cean, on the wide Pa - ci - fic shore, saw the queen of flow-ing

2. - 4. *See Additional Lyrics*

riv - ers, might-y moun-tain by the score. She's long and she's tall and hand-some, yes, she's loved by one and

all, she's a mod - ern com - bi - na - tion called the Wa - bash Can - non - ball. ball.

Additional Lyrics

2. Listen to the jingle, the rumble and the roar.
Riding through the woodlands, to the hills and by the shore.
Hear the mighty rush of the engine hear the lonesome hobo squall,
Riding through the jungle on the Wabash Cannonball.

3. Eastern states are dandies so the Western people say.
From New York to St. Louis and Chicago by the way.
Through the hills of Minnesota where the rippling waters fall,
No chances can be taken on the Wabash Cannonball.

4. Here's to Daddy Claxton, may his name forever stand.
May he ever be remembered through the parts of all our land.
When his earthly race is over and the curtain 'round him fall,
We'll carry him to glory on the Wabash Cannonball.

Wayfaring Stranger

Traditional American Folksong

Strum Pattern: 8
Pick Pattern: 8

Verse
Slowly

Oh, I'm a poor _____ way-far-in' stran-ger, _____

_____ trav-lin' through this world of woe. Yet there's no toil, _____

no sweat or dan-ger, _____ in that world to which I go.

Chorus

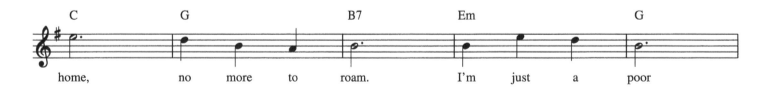

I'm go - ing home to see my lov'd ones, I'm go - ing

home, no more to roam. I'm just a poor

way-far-in' stran-ger, _____ going home, just go-ing home.

Water Is Wide

Traditional

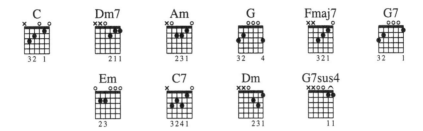

Strum Pattern: 2
Pick Pattern: 4

Modeartely

Verse

1. The wa - ter is wide, I can - not get o - ver,
2. - 5. See Additional Lyrics

and nei - ther have I wings to fly. _____ Give me a

boat _____ that can car - ry two, _____ and both shall

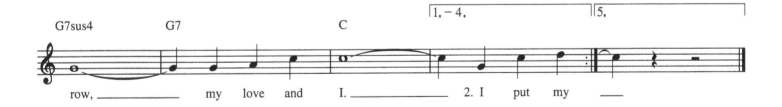

row, _____ my love and I. _____ 2. I put my _____

Additional Lyrics

2. I put my hand into some soft bush,
   Thinking the sweetest flower to find.
   The thorn, it stuck me to the bone,
   And oh, I left that flower alone.

3. A ship there is and she sails the sea,
   She's loaded deep as deep can be.
   But not so deep as the love I'm in,
   And I know not how to sink or swim.

4. Oh, love is handsome and love is fine,
   Gay as a jewel when first it's new.
   But love grows old and waxes cold,
   And fades away like summer dew.

5. I leaned my back against a young oak,
   Thinking he was a trusty tree.
   But first he bended and then he broke,
   And thus did my false love to me.

When Johnny Comes Marching Home

Words and Music by Patrick Sarsfield Gilmore (Louis Lambert)

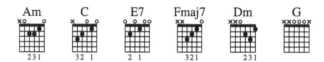

*Strum Pattern: 10
*Pick Pattern: 10

When John - ny comes march - ing home a - gain, hur - rah! _____ Hur -

one pattern per measure

rah! _____ We'll give him a heart - y wel - come then, hur - rah! _____ Hur -

rah! _____ Oh, the men will cheer and the boys will shout. The

la - dies they __ will all turn out. And we'll all feel gay when

John - ny comes march - ing home.

When the Saints Go Marching In

Words by Katherine E. Purvis
Music by James M. Black

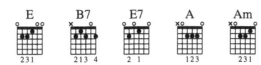

Strum Pattern: 1
Pick Pattern: 2

Brightly

Verse

1. Oh, when the saints _____ go march - ing in, _____
2. - 4. *See Additional Lyrics*

_____ oh, when the saints go march - ing in, _____

_____ oh Lord, I want to be in that

num - ber _____ when the saints go march - ing

1., 2., 3.
in. _____ 2. Oh, when the

4.
throne. _____

Additional Lyrics

2. Oh, when the sun refuse to shine,
   Oh, when the sun refuse to shine,
   Oh Lord, I want to be in that number,
   When the sun refuse to shine.

3. Oh, when they crown Him Lord of all,
   Oh, when they crown Him Lord of all,
   Oh Lord, I want to be in that number,
   When they crown Him Lord of all.

4. Oh, when they gather 'round the throne,
   Oh, when they gather 'round the throne,
   Oh Lord, I want to be in that number,
   When they gather 'round the throne.

Yankee Doodle

Traditional

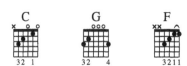

Strum Pattern: 10
Pick Pattern: 10

Verse
Moderately

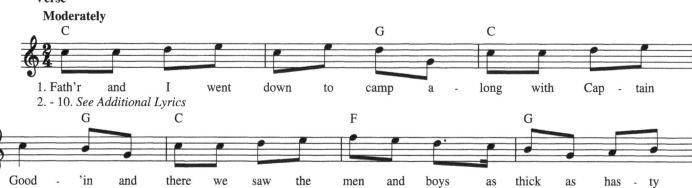

1. Fath'r and I went down to camp a - long with Cap - tain
2. - 10. *See Additional Lyrics*

Good - 'in and there we saw the men and boys as thick as has - ty

Chorus

pud - din'. Yan - kee Doo - dle keep it up, Yan - kee Doo - dle dan - dy.

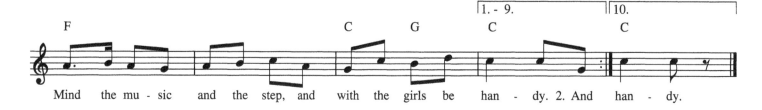

Mind the mu - sic and the step, and with the girls be han - dy. 2. And han - dy.

Additional Lyrics

2. And there we see a thousand men
   As rich as Squire David.
   And what they wasted ev'ry day
   I wish it could be saved.

3. And there was Captain Washington
   Upon a slapping stallion
   A-giving orders to his men,
   I guess there was a million.

4. And then the feathers on his hat,
   They looked so very fine, ah!
   I wanted peskily to get
   To give to my Jemima.

5. And there I see a swamping gun,
   Large as a log of maple,
   Upon a mighty little cart,
   A load for father's cattle.

6. And ev'ry time they fired it off,
   It took a horn of powder.
   It made a noise like father's gun,
   Only a nation louder.

7. An' there I see a little keg,
   Its head all made of leather.
   They knocked upon't with little sticks
   To call the folks together.

8. And Cap'n Davis had a gun,
   He kind o'clapt his hand on't
   And stuck a crooked stabbing-iron
   Upon the little end on't.

9. The troopers, too, would gallop up
   And fire right in ours faces.
   It scared me almost half to death
   To see them run such races.

10. It scared me so I hooked it off
    Nor stopped, as I remember,
    Nor turned about till I got home,
    Locked up in mother's chamber.

The Yellow Rose of Texas

Traditional Folksong

Strum Pattern: 3
Pick Pattern: 3

Lively — **Verse**

1. There's a yel-low rose in Tex-as that I am goin' to
3. *See Additional Lyrics*

see, no oth-er fel-low loves her, no-bod-y, on-ly

me. She cried so when I left her, it like to broke my

heart, and if I ev-er find __ her, we nev-er-more will

Verse

part. 2. She's the sweet-est rose of col-or this fel-low ev-er
4. *See Additional Lyrics*

knew, her eyes are bright as dia-monds they spar-kle like the dew. You may

talk a - bout your dear-est May, and sing of Ro - sa Lee, but the

1.
yel-low rose of Tex-as beats the belles of Ten - nes - see. 3. Where the

2.
more.

Additional Lyrics

3. Where the Rio Grande is flowing
   And the starry skies are bright,
   She walks along the river,
   In the quiet summer night.
   She thinks, if I remember,
   When we parted long ago,
   I promised to come back again,
   And not to leave her so.

4. Oh, now I'm goin' to find her,
   For my heart is full of woe,
   And we'll sing the song together,
   That we sang so long ago.
   We'll play the banjo gaily
   And we'll sing the songs of yore,
   And the yellow rose of Texas
   Shall be mine forevermore.

Your Favorite Music For Guitar Made Easy

American Folksongs For Easy Guitar

Over 70 songs, including: All The Pretty Little Horses • Animal Fair • Aura Lee • Billy Boy • Buffalo Gals (Won't You Come Out Tonight) • Bury Me Not On The Lone Prairie • Camptown Races • (Oh, My Darling) Clementine • (I Wish I Was In) Dixie • The Drunken Sailor • Franky And Johnny • Home On The Range • Hush, Little Baby • I've Been Working On The Railroad • Jacob's Ladder • John Henry • My Old Kentucky Home • She'll Be Comin' Round The Mountain • Shenandoah • Simple Gifts • Swing Low, Sweet Chariot • The Wabash Cannon Ball • When Johnny Comes Marching Home • and more!
00702031 ....$9.95

The Big Christmas Collection

An outstanding collection of 100 Christmas tunes that even beginners can enjoy. Songs include: Away In A Manger • The Chipmunk Song • Deck The Hall • Feliz Navidad • Frosty The Snow Man • Fum, Fum, Fum • Grandma's Killer Fruitcake • Happy Holiday • It's Beginning To Look Like Christmas • Rudolph, The Red-Nosed Reindeer • Silent Night • Silver Bells • You're All I Want For Christmas • and more.
00698978....................................$14.95

The Broadway Book

Over 100 favorite show tunes including: All I Ask Of You • Beauty And The Beast • Cabaret • Edelweiss • I Whistle A Happy Tune • Memory • One • People • Sound Of Music • Tomorrow • With One Look • and more.
00702015 .... $14.95

Children's Songs For Easy Guitar

Over 60 songs, including: Are You Sleeping • The Bare Necessities • Beauty And The Beast • The Brady Bunch • The Candy Man • Casper The Friendly Ghost • Edelweiss • Feed The Birds • (Meet) The Flintstones • Happy Trails • Heigh Ho • I'm Popeye The Sailor Man • Jesus Loves Me • The Muffin Man • On Top Of Spaghetti • Puff The Magic Dragon • A Spoonful Of Sugar • Zip-A-Dee-Doo-Dah • and more.
00702027 ....$12.95

The Classic Country Book

Over 100 favorite country hits including: Another Somebody Done Somebody Wrong Song • Could I Have This Dance • Don't It Make My Brown Eyes Blue • Elvira • Folsom Prison Blues • The Gambler • Heartaches By The Number • I Fall To Pieces • Kiss An Angel Good Mornin' • Lucille • The Most Beautiful Girl In The World • Oh, Lonesome Me • Rocky Top • Sixteen Tons • Tumbling Tumbleweeds • Will The Circle Be Unbroken • You Needed Me • and more.
00702018....................................$19.95

The Classic Rock Book

89 monumental songs from the '60's, '70's and '80's, such as: American Woman • Born To Be Wild • Cocaine • Dust In The Wind • Fly Like An Eagle • Gimme Three Steps • I Can See For Miles • Layla • Magic Carpet Ride • Reelin' In The Years • Sweet Home Alabama • Tumbling Dice • Walk This Way • You Really Got Me • and more.
00698977....................................$19.95

National Anthems For Easy Guitar

50 official national anthems in their original language, complete with strum and pick patterns and chord frames. Countries represented include Australia, Brazil, Canada, Cuba, France, Germany, Great Britain, Haiti, Irish Republic, Mexico, Peru, Poland, Russia, Sweden, United States of America, and more.
00702025 ....$12.95

The New Country Hits Book

100 hot country hits including: Achy Breaky Heart • Ain't Going Down ('Til The Sun Comes Up) • Blame It On Your Heart • Boot Scootin' Boogie • Chattahoochee • Don't Rock The Jukebox • Friends In Low Places • Honky Tonk Attitude • I Feel Lucky • I Take My Chances • Little Less Talk And A Lot More Action • Mercury Blues • One More Last Chance • Somewhere In My Broken Heart • T-R-O-U-B-L-E • The Whiskey Ain't Workin' • and more.
00702017....................................$19.95

FOR MORE INFORMATION, SEE YOUR LOCAL MUSIC DEALER, OR WRITE TO:

HAL•LEONARD® CORPORATION
7777 W. BLUEMOUND RD. P.O. BOX 13819 MILWAUKEE, WI 53213

Contact Hal Leonard on the internet at http://www.halleonard.com
Prices, contents, and availability subject to change without notice. Some products may not be available outside the U.S.A.